OUS TES

TERRY DEARY
ILLUSTRATED BY MARTIN BROWN

SCHOLAST   04662256

For Richard Smith with thanks and admiration. TD

Thanks Atholl. MB

Scholastic Children's Books,
Euston House, 24 Eversholt Street,
London NW1 1DB, UK

A division of Scholastic Ltd
London ~ New York ~ Toronto ~ Sydney ~ Auckland
Mexico City ~ New Delhi ~ Hong Kong

First published in the UK by Scholastic Ltd, 2006
(as *Horrible Histories Handbooks: Pirates*)
This edition published 2010

Text © Terry Deary, 2006
Illustrations © Martin Brown, Atholl McDonald 2006

ISBN 978 1407 11468 2

Printed and bound by Tien Wah Press Pte. Ltd, Malaysia

2 4 6 8 10 9 7 5 3 1

The right of Terry Deary, Martin Brown and Atholl McDonald to be identified as the author and
illustrator of this work respectively has been asserted by them in accordance with the Copyright,
Designs and Patents Act, 1988.

Papers used by Scholastic Children's Books are made from woods grown in sustainable forests.

Contents

Introduction

What do you call a person who takes you prisoner and feeds you rats, mice and caterpillars?

> A THUG?

What do you call a person who nails your feet to the deck of a ship and then beats you to death?

> A BULLY?

What do you call a person who chops you into pieces and eats you?

> A CANNIBAL?

There is one word for all of these vicious people ... **Pirates**

> A PIRATE? BUT I THOUGHT...

Yes, it's shocking but true.

Forget the handsome young men, sailing the seven seas, digging up hidden treasure.

Forget the brave heroes swinging from masts to steal the gold from enemy galleons and laughing as they swish their swords.

Forget the fat, jolly story-book captain and his cheeky parrot with an eye-patch.

ONE MORE YO-HO-HO AND I'LL FILL YOU FULL OF YO-HO-HOLES

For this is a **HORRIBLE** history of pirates. And not only that, but it's everything you **DON'T** want to know about pirates in one brilliant book.

So, avast and belay you lubber, shiver your timbers and weigh your anchor, me hearties.[1]

Read this book and you may never plough the seven seas again!

---

1 No, I don't know what that means either. Just shout it as you swing from the ropes in the school gym.

Lousy legends and lies

You've seen the movies, you've read the books. Pirates are brave and handsome young men (and women) who wear gold earrings and shiny boots. They carry swords and pistols but never hurt anyone ... except the baddies.

Here are ten 'facts' about story-book pirates. Can you say which of these are true?

If you think it may have happened say, **AYE, JIM LAD!**

If you think it was a lie then say,

NEVER, ME HEARTIES

1. Pirates were gentlemen thieves.

Answer: 'Aye, Jim lad!' Blackbeard was thought to be a 'learned' man born into a well-to-do family. Henry Morgan was made 'Sir Henry' by King Charles II and went on to be Governor of Jamaica. But some were not even men! Mary Read and Anne Bonney were a couple of tough women who swashed and buckled alongside the men.

2. Pirates carried parrots.

Answer: 'Aye, Jim lad!' The parrots were captured in South America and carried back home. But they weren't just cute pets – they could be sold for good money in Europe. Pretty Polly made a pretty penny.

3. Pirates stole Spanish gold and jewels.

Answer: 'Aye, Jim lad!' But the Spanish ships became too big and too well-armed. Pirates turned to stealing things they could sell – sugar and cloth were popular. Slaves made a good price. Never mind the misery.

4. Pirates made maps of buried treasure.

Answer: 'Never, me hearties.' They shared the money and spent it quickly. There was no point in burying it. Captain Kidd was supposed to have buried treasure but no one has ever found it. It's a daft thing to do with your loot when you think about it. The only pirates who buried their loot were the ones being chased by the navy. They would hide it for a couple of days till it was safe to move on.

5. Pirates marooned shipmates on desert islands.

Answer: 'Aye, Jim lad!' It was a punishment for a pirate who broke the rules. Believe it or not, pirates did have a set of rules – just like school rules! The rules even said what time you had to put your lights out and go to bed!

6. Pirates had wooden legs and eye-patches.

Answer: 'Aye, Jim lad!' Cannon shots could mangle legs and smash faces. A saw would take off a crushed leg and there was always wood to make a handy new stump – if stinking gangrene in the wound didn't kill you first.

TREASURE!
I'M RICH!
MAROONED...
BUT RICH!

7. Pirates flew skull-and-cross-bone flags.

Answer: 'Aye, Jim lad!' But other flags had bleeding hearts or daggers or whole skeletons on them. A lot of 'pirate' flags may have been invented long after the pirates were dead.

8. Pirates made enemies walk the plank.

Answer: 'Never, me hearties.' That was just for stories. Pirates never wasted their time. If they wanted enemies dead they just chopped them to pieces and fed them to the sharks. Chinese pirates may have made victims walk the plank – and one writer said Black Bart did it in the Caribbean. But that's probably not true. It may be true that they threw a victim into the sea and called out...

Sea rover

A polite word for a pirate. Call him this if he has a cutlass to your throat. Sea king is an even MORE polite word for a pirate – makes him sound like some posh hero. Really he's see-king to rob you.

ROVER IS A DOG'S NAME

Marooner

Marooner comes from the Spanish word 'cimarrona' and means a 'runaway'. These men were either runaway slaves or Spanish sailors who ran away from the cruel life on their treasure ships – they slaved away on the ships but didn't get a share of the treasure. No wonder they ran away. In time the word 'marooning' was used to mean leaving a victim on a deserted island – this is not the same as the purple colour known as maroon. And it has nothing at all to do with this awful joke...

I SAY! I SAY! I SAY! A SHIP FULL OF RED PAINT CRASHED INTO A SHIP FULL OF BLUE PAINT AND THEY SANK. THE CREW WERE MAROONED!

Freebooter

A Dutch word for thieves who roam around (freely) looking for loot (booty). Do not mix him up with a footballer who has an extra leg:

FREEBOOTER

THREE-BOOTER

Filibuster

Spanish word for a pirate. Useful if you are attacked while on holiday.

HAND OVER YOUR RUBBER RING

FILIBUSTER!

Top ten putrid pirates

Here's a quick guide to the pirates you would NOT want to see at sea or cross cutlasses with in a cabin.

Their horrors have been scored with skulls! A one-skull pirate is nasty – but a five-skull pirate is more deadly than a crocodile with toothache.

1 Blackbeard (Edward Teach, 1680–1718)

• He sometimes killed his own crew for sport. He shot his mate Israel Hands in the knee and crippled him for life, just for fun.

• He wore plaits in his beard and hair so it looked like snakes were crawling over his face and head. He also twisted smoking rope into the plaits to add to his terrifying looks.

• He was so strong he could split a man from his head to his waist with one blow from his cutlass.

Skull Score: ☠☠☠☠☠

I'M OFF

2 Sir Henry Morgan (1635–88)

• This Welshman started off as a privateer, attacking the Spanish for King Charles. He did such a good job Charles made him governor of Jamaica.

• Morgan was a good soldier but a hopeless sailor. He wrecked one ship by sailing it on to rocks. He had to cling to a rock and wait to be rescued. Embarrassing.

• Another of his ships blew up when some drunken sailors knocked a candle over in the gunpowder store. Morgan lived – 250 of his crew died.

Skull Score: 💀💀

3 Coxinga (1624–62)

• Coxinga was the son of China's richest smuggler. He fought to defend his emperor and built a navy of 3,000 ships and 250,000 fighting men. When the emperor was finally defeated Coxinga turned to piracy.

• He couldn't return to China so he decided to drive out the Dutch traders on Taiwan Island. The Dutch refused to surrender. Coxinga had the Dutch captives divided into groups of about 30 and sent to villages round his camp. There they were dragged out, killed and thrown into burial pits.

• Coxinga went mad and started screaming, 'Take those headless bodies out of my bedroom!' There was nothing there.

Skull Score: 💀💀💀

4 Black Bart (Bartholomew Roberts c. 1682–1722)

• Bart started his life at sea working on a slave ship. Then a pirate captured him and made Bart a slave. The hard-working Welshman earned his freedom and in time became captain of his own ship. Bart once captured a ship and asked the captain to pay if he wanted to go free. The captain refused so Bart set his ship on fire. It didn't bother Bart that there were eighty slaves on board.

• Black Bart was an odd pirate because he didn't drink - he had a clear head to plan his clever attacks. He also hated gambling and smoking on his ship.

• Bart found time to preach to his crew on a Sunday. His rule was 'Never attack on a Sunday, it is the Lord's Day.'

Skull Score: ☠☠☠

5 Ned Low (died c. 1724)

• This American pickpocket turned to pirating. He refused to have married men on his crew. He didn't want men running home to their wives. If a prisoner was married then he couldn't turn pirate – Low shot him in the head.

• Low captured the Spanish galleon *Montcova* and killed 53 Spanish captives with his cutlass. He made one Spanish prisoner eat the heart of his friend, then he killed him. He burnt a French cook alive. Low told him...

- His own crew set him adrift in a small boat. A French ship rescued him. When they found out who he was they hanged him.

Skull Score: ☠☠ ☠☠ ☠☠ ☠☠ ☠☠

6 Jeanne de Clisson (c. 1300s)

- In 1313 Jeanne's husband, Olivier de Clisson, was executed on the orders of Philip the Fair, King of France. Jeanne decided he was Philip the Un-fair and decided to get her own back. First she sold off all her lands to raise money, then she bought three warships; they were painted black and had red sails. Admiral Jeanne began destroying Philip's ships and murdering their crews ... but she always left two or three alive to carry the story back to the King. After all, that was part of the fun!

- Philip died – which could have spoilt Jeanne's fun but she decided to continue her revenge on his sons as they took the French throne. After 13 bloody years the last son of Philip died and Jeanne retired.

- It was said that she enjoyed capturing ships with French noblemen on board. Then she would personally chop off their heads with her axe. Her grey ghost still walks the walls of Clisson Castle – don't go there if your name is Philip!

Skull Score: ☠☠ ☠☠ ☠☠ ☠☠

7 Roche Brasiliano (1670s)

- This Dutch buccaneer lived in Brazil, then turned up in Jamaica in the 1670s to do some pirating.
- Brasiliano was a drunkard famous for his hatred of the Spanish. He would get drunk and run down the street beating anyone who got in his way.
- He soon became pirate captain and brought terror to Spanish shipping. His nastiest trick was to capture a Spaniard, tie him to a pole and roast him alive over a fire.

Skull Score: 💀💀💀💀

8 Juan Corso (1680s)

- The Spanish were not just victims of piracy. Some Spaniards, like Juan Corso, became pirates themselves — and cruel ones too.
- Corso became a Spanish privateer with orders to destroy the English in Jamaica. He gathered a crew of killers who robbed and murdered without pity.
- One of Corso's crew fell sick. He was not able to row Corso's boat. He was useless ... so Corso cut off his head.

Skull Score: 💀💀💀

9 Lady Mary Killigrew (1580s)

• This cut-throat woman was the wife of Sir John Killigrew and they lived in Cornwall. She went on many pirating cruises along the English coast and was happy to slash and chop with her own sword. In 1583 a German merchant ship was robbed and she rowed away with jewels, silver and pieces of eight. After killing the crew, of course.

• In the same year a Spanish merchant ship was driven into Falmouth by storms. Lady Killigrew led a boarding party on to the vessel, killed the crew and stole the cargo.

• Queen Elizabeth I heard about the attack and was furious. Lady Killigrew was tried and sentenced to be hanged along with her crew. But at the last minute the Queen, who liked Lady Killigrew, changed her mind and gave her a long jail sentence instead.

Skull Score: ☠☠ ☠☠ ☠☠ ☠☠

10 François l'Olonoise (1660s)

• L'Olonoise, a French pirate, brought terror to the coast of South America… He tortured his prisoners and became famous as the cruellest of all pirates.

• His nastiest habit was cutting prisoners to bits when he lost his temper. Then he would cut out their tongues. Once he cut out a prisoner's heart and starting chewing it while asking him questions.

• L'Olonoise was wrecked on the island of Las Pertas. He was found by local natives and was murdered in a horrible way. Served him right.

Skull Score: ☠ ☠ ☠ ☠ ☠

Perilous pirate timeline

To give you a rough idea of who was doing what and when, here is a quick timeline...

Around 1100 BC The first pirates roam the Mediterranean seas.

230 BC Queen Teuta of Illyria (that's Albania today) is fed up with the Greeks settling on the coast of her country. She hasn't the forces to drive them out of their towns so she turns pirate to sink them at sea. But when she tries to be ruthless with Roman ships she is defeated.

Vikings cross the North Sea and slaughter monks.

AD 793 It's the start of the Viking age. They will spill blood on land and sea for more than three hundred years.

AD 401 St Patrick (AD 385–461) was a British boy who was taught the Bible by his dad. When St Pat was sixteen he was captured by pirates and sold as a slave in Ireland. After six years he

Wicked weapons

If you want to be a pirate you need to have plenty of weapons. You will want to stab, shoot, smash down doors, chop through ropes and burn sails.

Here are some usual – and unusual – weapons for you to wear.

Cutlass

Why did pirates like the curvy 'cutlass' sword? Because there were lots of ropes on a sailing ship. The curved sword didn't get tangled in the ropes. Unless you used it the wrong way round, of course...

Brass knife

Salty water makes iron and steel rot and rust. A brass knife would stay sharp. It was usually short and sharp for cutting and stabbing. (It is also useful for picking your teeth if you've forgotten to pack your corsair toothbrush. Just don't use it to pick your nose.)

FOR SALE
ONE NOT-SO-
CAREFUL OWNER

Axe

If you want an enemy ship to stop then chop the ropes that hold up the sails. The sails will collapse and fall on the crew. Pirate axes were around 70 cm long and weighed about a kilo. An axe is useful for a quick chop. And a quick chop is very nice – especially if it's a lamb chop.

Tar bomb

Wrap a lump of tar, the size of your head, around a rope. When the enemy is close, set fire to the tar and use the rope to throw it on to the enemy deck or sails. It will stick and set fire to their ship. They won't be able to pull it off. While the crew try to put out the fire you jump aboard and attack them. Just make sure you don't step on one of your own tar bombs when you leap aboard.

Flintlock pistols

These pistols were used by Caribbean pirates but they weren't deadly. They were noisy and made clouds of smoke but were not very accurate. They took a long time to load and often didn't fire at all. Pirates like Blackbeard carried a dozen of them stuffed into his belt to save time. One of them would work sooner or later – or you could always throw them at your enemy.

Marlin spikes

These metal spikes with handles were not meant to be weapons but tools for working on ropes.

But the captain would lock the guns and cutlasses away until you went into battle. What could you use if you wanted to attack the captain? The marlin spike was a handy weapon.

Grappling hooks

Iron hooks on the end of a long rope. Throw them across to an enemy ship and pull on the rope. The other ship won't be able to sail away from you. It's a bit like a spider trapping a fly.

Buccaneer knives

Buccaneers in the Caribbean enjoyed hunting wild pigs or boars. They were expert shots but DIDN'T use their guns to kill the pigs. They enjoyed the 'sport' of running after the boar and chopping it down with their long sharp knives. Each buccaneer had at least two large knives. These knives were shorter than a cutlass. The aim was to slice the back legs of the pig so it couldn't run. They would then jump it from behind and slit its throat.

Duck's foot

If you want to shoot someone use a duck's foot. This was a pistol with FOUR barrels. You could fire all four at the same time so you were sure to hit something. The barrels were joined together and looked a little like a duck's foot. You'd be quackers not to use one!

...and one weapon to use AGAINST a pirate attack:

Cows

In 1670 Panama City was under attack. The Spanish governor wasn't too worried because he had a secret weapon ... a herd of cows, trained to charge at the English enemy.

The English were led by the famous Welsh pirate, Sir Henry Morgan. His men were exhausted. On the march to Panama they were so starved they had to eat their own boots. Morgan's men charged. The Spanish set the cows loose ... but they were scared by the pirates. They turned around and charged the Spanish by mistake. Oo-oops! (Or should that be moo-oops?) The Spanish fled but burned the city so Morgan went back with nothing. Still, at least they had cows to eat. Tastier than boots.

YUM!

☠ DID YOU KNOW…? ☠

If you were a trader and afraid of pirates how could you defend your ship? Put cannon on board? But it was hard to find good gunners – they were either in the navy or on pirate ships. And a cannon is no good without a gunner. So some ship-owners painted pictures of cannon on the sides of their ships and hoped it would scare the pirates away.

TERRIBLE TACTICS

You can't just jump on a ship and sail off looking for other ships to attack. Pirates had special ways of doing things – tactics.

RANSOM A SHIP

Capture a ship and sell it back to the owner. That saves you taking the captured ships to port, selling the treasure and killing the crew.

Black Bart, a Welshman, was a good sailor and fighter. He terrorized the ships in the Caribbean and off the Guinea coast. In one raid he captured eleven ships and sold ten back to their owners.

FAKE FEMALES

The easiest way to capture a ship is to get yourself invited on board. Once you are on the deck you pull out your weapons and surprise the crew.

But how do you trick the victims? After all, no one would invite a pirate on board their ship.

A painter called Auguste Francois Biard painted a picture of pirates taking a ship. The pirates are all dressed as women. We don't know if it really happened, but if it did, it was crafty.

HOW'S ME LIPPY?

ARRR! THAT BE FINE. 'TIS YOUR EYE-LINER THAT'S A MESS

'Bess' … if she'd really been a pirate she'd have been Hanger Bess!

• Gertie's story was made up by a teacher who told it to her class. She sent it to a newspaper as an April fool joke. A lot of people believe it and say there really WAS a Gunpowder Gertie. There wasn't.

• Maria Cobham and her husband were probably completely made up.

• Charlotte's story was first printed in 1836. Many people believe it. Yet it is too daft to be true.

• Alwilda's story was probably half truth, half legend.

Cut-throat cruelties

Pirates were tough on their enemies ... and tough on their friends. Many sailors worked on trading ships and learned to hate the cruel captains. When a sailor turned to piracy he would make sure the trader captain suffered most of all. They would sometimes question the captured crew...

If the answer was 'No' then the captain could die.

Pirate Phillip Lyne said in 1726 that he had murdered 37 captains. That was not the only cruelty that went on at sea…

Moses' Law

The Bible said that 40 lashes of a whip would kill a man. If a pirate captain wanted to punish a man – but not kill him – he would order 39 lashes. The truth is a weak man could easily die from 20 lashes. There are also reports of sailors being lashed 100 times and living.

The Romans also used the 39-lash rule. But their whips had 12 strands and lead weights in the end or even hooks. It tore the skin and flesh off the back. The sailors' 'cat-o'-nine tails' whips had nine strands with knots at the end.

Chinese choppers
Some Chinese pirates were very cruel. Captives were crushed into tiny cabins then fed on rats, mice and caterpillars.

Some reports say Chinese pirates nailed their prisoners' feet to the deck. Then they beat them to death, cut them up and ate them.

Ruthless rovers
The Gujarati rovers were the most feared pirates in the Indian Ocean. When they sailed the west coast of India they took their families with them.

If they captured someone who had no treasure they thought the victim might have swallowed it. So they forced prisoners to swallow tamarind root to make them vomit up any jewels.

Earache
Pirate queen Ching Shih did not like her sailors to desert. If they were caught she had their ears sliced off and shown to the other sailors as a lesson.

But that was kind compared to what pirate Ned Low did when he captured a Nantucket whaling ship. He made her captain eat his own sliced-off ears, sprinkled with salt. Then he killed him.

Sew cruel
Dutch pirate Dirk Chivers captured two ships in 1695. Captain Sawbridge was one of those taken prisoner. Sawbridge was not happy. Sawbridge moaned ... and moaned ... and moaned. Chivers was so fed up with his moaning he took a sail needle and sewed up Sawbridge's mouth.

Pitiless pirates
Some Cuban pirates captured the English ship *Eliza Ann*. A woman called Lucretia Parker wrote to her brother to tell the tale of what happened to the crew…

First they took off all of the crew's clothes except their shirts and trousers. Then they attacked them with swords, knives and axes. They were as ferocious as cannibals. They ignored pleas for mercy as the crew begged the murderers to spare their lives. Our Captain Smith tried to win the pirates' pity by telling them of his wife and three small children. But he was pleading with monsters who have no human feelings. After receiving a heavy blow from an axe he snapped the cords he was bound with and, trying to escape, he was met by another of the ruffians who plunged a knife into his heart. I was standing near him at the time and was covered with his blood. On receiving the wound he gave a single groan and fell, lifeless, at my feet. Dear brother, I don't need to paint a picture of my feelings at that awful moment!

Luckily a British warship appeared before they could turn on Lucretia. The pirates abandoned the *Eliza Ann* and she was saved. They were arrested later in Jamaica.

Lucretia Parker identified them and had the pleasure of watching them hang.

Rotten rules

Pirates may seem lawless but they often had their own rules: 'The Pirate Articles'.

Just like proper laws, you had to obey or be punished.

Sometimes pirates captured a trading ship and gave the crew a choice…

Sometimes they killed anyone who refused to sign. These are the 'Pirate Articles'. Would you sign them … or die?

Every man on the crew has an equal vote on their action and an equal share of food and drink on the ship. The Captain shall receive two persons' share of any treasure.

✠

All men shall have an equal share of treasure. Any man who takes more than his share of gold or jewels or money shall be punished by marooning.

✠

No person shall play cards or dice for money.

✠

Lights and candles shall be put out at eight o'clock each night.

✠

Each person must make sure his own pistol and cutlass are well kept and ready for use at all times.

✠

No boy or woman shall be allowed on board the ship when she sails. Any man carrying a woman to sea shall suffer death[3].

✠

Any person who deserts the ship in a battle shall suffer death or marooning.

✠

There shall be no fighting on board ship. All quarrels shall be settled on the shore with sword and cutlass.

✠

No person shall talk of leaving the crew until everyone has shared at least a thousand pounds.

✠

The ship's musicians shall be allowed to rest on a Sunday.

BUT ... there wasn't just ONE pirate code. The one above was written by Black Bart – other pirates had other rules.

3 But what about women pirates? This is an actual document – ask the writer!

☠ Pirate ships ☠

If you're going to be a pirate then you need to give your ship a terrifying name. You would NOT want to call your ship something sweet like Blessing ... but pirate Captain Brown did. Which is your favourite from these deadly days of the Caribbean pirates?

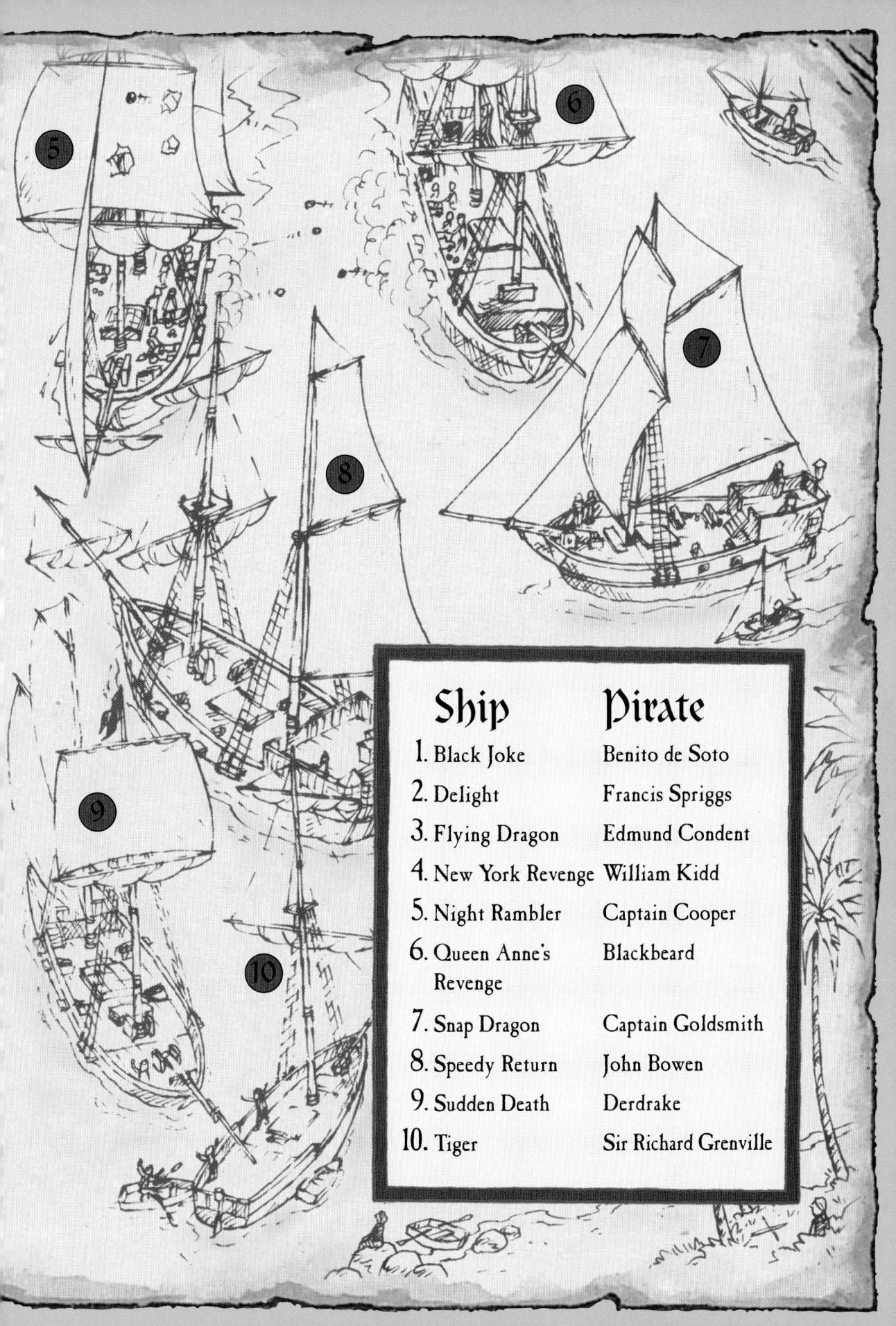

Ship   Pirate

1. Black Joke   Benito de Soto
2. Delight   Francis Spriggs
3. Flying Dragon   Edmund Condent
4. New York Revenge   William Kidd
5. Night Rambler   Captain Cooper
6. Queen Anne's   Blackbeard
   Revenge
7. Snap Dragon   Captain Goldsmith
8. Speedy Return   John Bowen
9. Sudden Death   Derdrake
10. Tiger   Sir Richard Grenville

Pirate losers

Not many pirates lived an exciting and happy life. Most of them were simple criminals with a rough life and an unhappy end.

Captain Hiram Breakes (born 1745)

Breakes was a Dutch sailor who fell in love with a woman called Mrs Snyde. Soon afterwards Mr Snyde died ... from poison. Breakes and Mrs Snyde were tried. Mrs Snyde said she didn't do it and they got away with murder.

Then Breakes stole his boss's ship and used it to attack a treasure ship from Chile. He had the crew murdered.

He said…

DEAD MEN TELL NO TALES

This was not a very clever thing to say. (Pirate Erik Cobham said pretty much the same thing, 'Dead cats don't meow.')

When he went back to Holland he found Mrs Snyde had tried to poison their baby son and had been hanged. Breakes was so upset he threw himself off a Dutch dyke and drowned himself.

You COULD say ... Snyde died; Mrs Snyde tried; Mrs Snyde lied; Baby Snyde died, Mrs Snyde tried; Mrs Snyde died; Breakes cried.

Abraham Cooke (1611–48)

This Welshman went to the Caribbean to herd cattle. He killed the cattle and sold the meat to the Spanish treasure ships. Then he discovered it was better to rob those ships.

He and his men stole so much treasure they built houses at Port Royal with doors of gold. Then Cooke sailed into a trap. He attacked a Spanish trading ship which was filled with Spanish soldiers and Cooke died in the fighting.

Cyril Hood (died 1648)

Cyril Hood was a useless buccaneer. In 1648 he gave up pirating and decided to make some money by betraying his old pirate pals.

Hood went to a Spanish captain and said, 'I know where the next attack is planned – pay me one hundred gold pieces and I'll tell you.' The Spanish captain didn't believe sad Cyril and refused to pay. So horrible Hood said, 'All right, give me a bottle of rum and I'll tell you.' This time the captain agreed. Cyril Hood betrayed buccaneer Abraham Cooke. Cooke got killed – Hood got drunk. Cooke's cousin Abel got hold of Hood and hanged him from the mast of his ship.

Rachel Wall (1760–89)

Around the age of 16, blue-eyed Rachel took a trip to Pennsylvania for the funeral of her grandfather. While wandering the docks she met a shady fisherman by the name of George Wall. She soon married him, and the two of them went to live in Boston.

The hungry couple stole a ship and began pirating off the Isle of Shoals. They tricked passing ships by pretending to be in trouble. 'Oh, help us!' pretty Rachel would cry. Once they had robbed their victims they would sink the captured ships and drown everyone aboard.

Then in 1782 George was washed away in a storm. Rachel made a living by creeping on board ships in the harbour and raiding the cabins. She was good at it. But in 1789 she was caught and tried. At the age of 29 she was hanged.

William Fly (died 1726)

Fly was a boxer before he joined a pirate ship. He led a mutiny and captured the captain. 'Jump or we'll throw you overboard.' The captain was thrown. Fly took over and was a pitiless master – he had many men lashed with a hundred lashes.

Fly was a hopeless sailor and managed to capture just one ship before his crew mutinied. They didn't throw him overboard. They handed him over for hanging.

At least Fly enjoyed his execution. He stood on the gallows, holding bunches of flowers, smiling and waving. The noose wasn't very well made so Fly tied the knot properly before slipping it over his head.

John Quelch (died 1704)

In 1703, John Quelch set off on the privateer *Charles*. He didn't like the captain much so, shortly after leaving the dock, Quelch tossed him overboard. He headed for the south Atlantic, as a privateer to rob French and Spanish ships.

Not long afterwards he came across a Portuguese gold ship and robbed her. Big mistake. England was at peace with Portugal and was not allowed to attack their ships.

The English navy wanted to show Portugal how sorry they were. Quelch was captured, taken back to Maine and hanged.

Nicholas Brown (died 1726)

In the 1700s, Brown was a pirate attacking ships around Jamaica. He was caught and sentenced to hang. But the King spared his life if he promised to give up piracy.

Brown, however, did go back to piracy and became known as 'The Grand Pirate'. Now the British Navy set out to hunt him down. The man who caught Brown was his old school pal, John Drudge. In 1726, Drudge killed Brown … then chopped off his head and pickled it. He took the head back to Britain to claim the reward.

Rahmah bin Jabr (1756–1826)

Rahmah made himself the most famous pirate of the Persian Gulf. He started off badly, losing one eye in a battle, but he raided ships for 50 years and lived to the age of 70.

This piratical pensioner should have stopped there and lived to 80. But he upset the people of Bahrain so much they sent all of their navy after him. Rahmah knew he was beaten. He let his enemies close in on him. Then he set fire to the gunpowder store on his own ship. He blew up many enemy ships … the bits of bin Jabr must have enjoyed that.

Manuel Pardal Rivero (died 1670)

Manuel was from Portugal but became a privateer for Spain. The trouble was he wasn't a very good pirate. In his first raid he sailed for the English fleet in Jamaica … but the wind changed and he attacked Grand Cayman instead. He landed at a poor village, stole two boats, captured four children and sailed off.

He finally reached Jamaica and called the governor, Sir Henry Morgan, to come out and fight. Morgan sailed off and attacked Panama instead and Manuel couldn't stop him. At last he did meet the English ship of Captain John Morris. Manuel's crew jumped overboard – they drowned or were shot as they swam ashore. Sir Henry Morgan chased Manuel along the beach and shot him dead.

Captain William Kidd (1645–1701)

In 1696 Captain Kidd was sent to the Indian Ocean with the job of catching pirates. Rich men in America gave him the money to buy a ship. But those men hoped he would really be robbing and bringing them back a fortune.

Kidd did capture a rich prize, the *Quedah Merchant*, but decided to share most of his loot with his crew instead. He hid the rest on an island. The rich Americans were furious. When he returned he was arrested and found guilty of piracy. He was sent back to England to hang.

He was hanged twice – the rope broke the first time. Then he was hanged in chains till his body rotted. Kidd died. His rich 'friends' lived on.

And one pirate winner…

Red Legs Greaves c. 1670–80

Red Legs Greaves was from a Scottish slave family. He escaped and joined the cruel Captain Hawkins as a Caribbean pirate. But Red Legs refused to torture or kill prisoners. His bare Scottish legs burned in the sun and that's how he got his name.

Red Legs made a fortune in one raid on a Spanish fortress. He retired to Nevis Island but was betrayed and arrested and sentenced to hang. Then an earthquake on Nevis destroyed the jail and Red Legs was one of the few who lived. Lucky Red Legs.

Kindly Red Legs turned pirate-hunter and was given a pardon. He died of old age, very rich and loved by many people. Maybe the kindly pirate deserved his good luck.

JO-HO-HO

Talk like a pirate

If a pirate shouted at you...

AVAST YE. YOU'VE GOT HAIRY WILLY ON ME SLOPS, YOU SCURVY LUBBER

Would you know what he was talking about? Probably not. Here are ten words to help you...

Want a ship to stop? Then call out 'heave to' because that means 'stand still'. It has nothing to do with 'heaving overboard' ... which is what you'd do if you found an enemy on your ship...

I CAN'T SWIM! I'LL DROWN

DON'T WORRY— THE SHARKS WILL EAT YOU LONG BEFORE THAT!

That dried fish may not look very tasty but it's better than nothing. Just remember you're eating something pirates call Hairy Willy.

HAIRY WILLY

SLOPS

Slops were the 1700s sailor word for trousers. Sailors were among the first people to wear trousers. Some went down to the ankles, some just below the knees.

A 'lubber' is a clumsy person on a ship. He'd be happier on land. If you really want a cutlass up your nose then call a pirate a 'landlubber'.

LANDLUBBER

Fly the flags

If you want to be a pirate then get a flag. Every pirate crew had its own flag – usually with skeletons, skulls, bones and swords.

The pirate flag was often called the 'Jolly Roger' – that is from the French 'jolie rouge' or 'pretty red'.

The first pirate flags were red. The other name for the pirate flag was:

Captain Death

The black flag may have been a signal that meant…

GIVE UP AND WE WILL LET YOU LIVE

If the victim tried to escape then the red flag was raised. That meant…

OK, CHAPS, WE'RE GOING TO KILL YOU

Here are a few of Captain Death's jolly flags:

John Avery ('Long Ben')
Probably the first to fly Captain Death around 1694. His ship was called The Fancy – fancy that! He died a poor beggar back in England.

Richard Worley
He robbed around the end of 1718 off the coast of New York. He invented the Jolly Roger flag with the skull and cross bones – the most popular flag. The British Navy caught him, took him ashore in North Carolina and hanged him.

Edward England
Invented the skull over crossed bones flag. Around 1720 he roamed the coasts of Africa and was murderous in Madagascar. He probably had a wooden leg and a wild beard. He could have been the real 'Long John Silver' from the book 'Treasure Island.'

Calico Jack Rackham

Calico Jack swapped the cross bones for cross cutlasses. His name was used for characters in movies such as 'Cut-throat Island' and 'Pirates of the Caribbean'. In the end, when the navy came to get him, he gave up without a fight. Some hero.

Blackbeard (aka Edward Teach, Edward Thatch)

Blackbeard started off by robbing for the king as a privateer. After a while he got fed up with giving up his loot to the mean monarch. He kept the cash and that made him a pirate. On his flag a skeleton-devil is holding an hourglass meaning, 'Your time is running out!' It is about to stab a bleeding heart.

Ned Low

Nasty Ned had a smart red skeleton on his flag. This meant, 'I mean business - make no bones about it.' He was last seen pirating round Africa in 1724. He's probably just a red skeleton by now.

Black Bart

Black Bart (Bartholomew Roberts) hated the governors of Barbados and Martinique. So he had their heads put on his flag as a warning ... Black Barty designed a flag, portraying a giant figure of himself standing, sword in hand, astride two skulls labelled A.B.H. ('a Barbadian's head') and A.M.H. ('a Martinican's head').

Horrible Histories note: Never mind how much you hate the school governors, don't try this at school ... or at skull.

ABH AMH

Thomas Tew

His Captain Death was a simple message ... 'This is what you're going to get if you don't give up quietly.' This flag was seen everywhere from America to the Mediterranean in Europe. But the cutlass didn't save him when a cannon shot blew him to pieces.

Emanuel Wynne

This French pirate copied the rest. The skull, the cross bones AND the hourglass. You may notice the hourglass is full at both ends – it will never run out. Maybe the message was, 'If you don't give up then I warn you, you'll die of old age!'

Christopher Moody

Christopher Moody attacked ships off the coast of Carolina between 1713 and 1718. He may not be famous as a pirate but he is remembered for his colourful flag.

Henry Morgan

The most horrible flag, to the Spanish, was this one. It is the Union Jack, flown by British ships from 1606 to 1801. When Britain was at war with Spain, privateers like Henry Morgan flew it as they attacked Spanish galleons. Naughty Morgan even attacked the Spanish when Britain were at PEACE with them! Well, a privateer has to make a living.

HORRIBLE HISTORIES
WARNING:

SOME of these flags may have been invented in pirate tales. Not many pirate flags have been found. MOST of these could be fake or made up by writers.

Foul facts

1 Pirates were often at sea for a long time so they took hens along (for eggs and meat). They also took 'hardtack' biscuits and limes. Their meat was often full of maggots and their biscuits were alive with weevils. They brushed some off and swallowed the rest.

2 On one island pirates were short of food so they had to eat snakes and monkeys.

3 When they needed to go to the loo they used a rope cage hanging over the sea.

4 When pirates buried treasure they would sometimes murder a prisoner and bury him on top of the treasure. That way the prisoner's ghost would guard the treasure. A sort of spook-curity guard. If they didn't have a prisoner then they might kill a member of the crew.

There was a sensible reason for this too. If the law came looking for the treasure they would say ...

A FRESH PILE OF EARTH, THEIR TREASURE IS THERE!

9 The captain was in charge of the ship and you had to obey him in a battle. But when the crew were not fighting they could vote to have a new captain.

A 'good' pirate captain was one who helped his crew win lots of treasure.

A 'bad' pirate captain was usually a dead pirate captain.

10 The worst job on a pirate ship was the job of 'powder monkey'. In a battle the powder monkey had to keep the gunners supplied with gunpowder. The job was usually given to boys about 11 or 12 years old – too young to fight with swords and pistols.

They were often kidnapped from their parents and forced to work. They were the youngest on the ship and the most bullied.

Powder monkey misery.

Pirate punishments

It was all very well being a pirate – roaming the seas and bashing people – until you were caught. Then you were treated with little pity.

HANGING

Pirates who were caught were usually hanged. In the 1700s this was a slow and horrible way to die.

In London the hangings didn't take place at the usual jails. The pirates were hanged at the docks where sailors could watch and cheer … or fear. The place was known as Execution Dock.

When the tide came in the bodies went under the water. After three soakings they were cut down.

Pirates were afraid of being hanged. If they were not given a proper burial they thought their spirits would go to hell. So some chose to die rather than be captured.

Two of Ned Low's pirates were terrified when a navy ship chased them. But they could not kill themselves – that was against their religion too. They would go to hell!

So each agreed to stand toe to toe, put a pistol to his friend's head and each would kill the other.

The ship escaped just in time. That saved someone having to mop brains off the deck.

HANGING IN CHAINS

The pirate's dead body would often be left swinging in the wind to teach people a lesson.

In 1704 Captain Quelch and five of his crew were hanged in Boston, USA. In case you couldn't get to see the bodies in chains a poet wrote about it for you...

I FEEL ROTTEN

> *You pirates who against God's laws did fight,*
> *Have all been hanged, which is very right,*
> *Some of you were old and some were young,*
> *And on the Boston gallows they were hung.*

Captain Kidd's dead body was painted with tar so it wouldn't rot. The black corpse was hung in a cage by the river Thames.

☠ DID YOU KNOW...? ☠

If a pirate was captured he would usually be taken to the nearest port for hanging. But he wasn't given a comfortable trip. Sometimes he'd be bound with ropes then hung up with the sails to swing in the wind.

BURIED FACE DOWN

The executed pirate was often buried on the seashore near where he was executed.

He wasn't buried in a churchyard because then his spirit would go to heaven.

Just to be extra sure his spirit stayed lost for ever, he was buried face down.

BURNED AT THE STAKE

Pirates in North Africa often captured Arab prisoners. The pirates were Christians (sort of) while the Arabs were Muslims. So the pirates forced the Arab Muslims to become Arab Christians ... or die.

The trouble was the Muslims hated the Arab Christians more than anything. If one was captured by his old Arab friends he faced an extra-nasty punishment ... he was burned alive.

BURIED ALIVE

Pirates lived by the sea and some died by the sea.

Welsh pirate Colyn Dolphyn was trapped at St Donats on the south coast of Wales. He was buried in the sand up to his neck. The tide came in slowly and he drowned.

DRY IN THE SUN

At Dead Man's Cay, near Kingston, Jamaica, pirates were executed by being fastened in an iron cage and hung up on a post to 'dry in the sun'.

Of course, after a slow and painful day they would 'die in the sun'.

The cage was made to fit tight round the pirate so his bones wouldn't fall away when his flesh rotted. Skeletons could hang there for years.

A REAL DRAG

One popular sort of punishment was to drag a pirate along behind a ship on a length of rope until he begged for mercy, drowned or was eaten by sharks. (A lot of people PAY to have this done to them today. They call it water-skiing.)

A THOUSAND CUTS

The Chinese had the most vicious punishment for pirate Nicholas Iquan. It was a slow death called 'death of a thousand cuts':

• A knife made a cut in the flesh, then the wound was sealed with a hot iron.

• This was done hundreds of times, working from the hands and feet towards the heart.

Just to make it worse for Iquan he had to watch this execution carried out on his two sons.

GRUB UP

A pirate prisoner held below deck on a pirate ship could be offered some disgusting food – grubs, beetles or cockroaches. They would have some slimy water to wash them down with. It was either eat the grubby grub or starve.

BOLT UP

An odd punishment for a pirate was to have iron bolts jammed into his mouth.

Dire deaths

Pirates didn't belong to any country. So any country could capture a pirate crew and punish them. If you were lucky they took away your ship. If you were unlucky you met a nastier end...

Caesar's pirates

Around 75 BC young Julius Caesar was on his way to Rhodes when the ship he was on was captured by pirates. The pirates said they'd set him free if his family paid 20 talents (gold pieces).

Julius was upset...

I'M GOING TO BE AN EMPEROR, I'M WORTH MORE THAN THAT. ASK FOR AT LEAST 50 TALENTS

So the pirates asked his parents for 50 and got it. He was set free.

Big mistake.

Years later Caesar hunted them down and had them all crucified.

He was a little cross – they got a great big cross.

Benito de Soto

Ruthless de Soto was caught in Gibraltar and sentenced to hang in 1832.

He was sent off to Cadiz to be hanged along with his crew. He arrived in Cadiz along with his coffin. A gallows was built on one of the docks and the death was a cruel one.

The pirate was brought to the gallows on a donkey cart and had to sit on his own coffin. When he reached the gallows he had the noose put around his neck and the cart would pull away leaving the pirate to strangle slowly. De Soto did not want to die that way. He stood on top of his coffin, reached for the rope and put the noose around his neck. He smiled to the crowd and cried:

You don't need me to tell you what that means.

You do? Oh, very well, it means, 'So long everybody!'

He jumped from the cart to his death. It was still slow and painful – but at least he went in style.

Black Bart

Bart was probably the cleverest pirate ever to set sail. He captured over 400 ships and took £50,000,000 in loot. He was killed in 1722 during a battle with an English warship off the coast of Africa. Half his throat was torn away by a cannon blast. His crew dumped his body overboard so that he would not be taken prisoner alive or dead.

There were 254 on his ship, including 70 African slaves and 18 French sailors all of whom he had forced into piracy. They may have been glad to see him dead … but not for long. After the defeat 52 were hanged.

Bart's motto was…

A SHORT LIFE BUT A MERRY ONE

Thomas Tew

Thomas Tew roamed across the Atlantic, Mediterranean and even the Red Sea.

His end came around 1695 during a sea battle with an Indian ship. An enemy cannon fired small pieces of metal at his ship – not the usual cannon ball. These shredded Tew's belly and his guts started to fall out on to the deck. He lay screaming in agony. His crew became so terrified by the sight that they gave up without another shot being fired.

William Lewis

In 1727 Lewis was chasing a rich treasure ship and it was getting away from him. He climbed the mast and began to tear out his own hair. He screamed…

Good devil – take this until we meet in hell!

Sure enough his ship speeded up and caught the treasure ship.

But Lewis's crew were terrified. 'He has made a deal with the Devil – the Devil will take him … and then he'll come for us!'

They decided that Lewis had to die.

That night they crept into his cabin and stabbed him to death.

He went to hell sooner than he thought.

☠ DID YOU KNOW...? ☠

Eustace was a Dutch monk in the 1200s. He gave up God and made a deal with the Devil (they said). The Devil gave Eustace the power to make his ship invisible.

It didn't do Eustace much good. He was beaten in a sea battle in 1217 and his head was cut off.

BEHOLD THE HEAD OF A PIRATE – I THINK

Captain George Lowther

In 1722, Lowther pulled his ship, *Happy Delivery*, up on to a beach to scrape the bottom clean. A navy ship came along and Lowther's crew were trapped on the island, Blanquilla, near Venezuela.

Lowther jumped through a cabin window and ran off to hide on the deserted island.

But he couldn't last long with no food or water. At last the navy found his corpse.

There was an empty pistol in its hand and a bullet through its brain.

Captain Morgan

Sir Henry Morgan gave up pirating and became governor of Jamaica in 1674. But he was bored and drank endless glasses of rum to pass the time. This destroyed his liver and he lay dying. Morgan swelled like a balloon and turned yellow.

The doctor only knew one cure — he had Morgan covered from head to toe in wet mud.

It didn't work. Morgan died, brown and sticky.

Blackbeard

In 1718, Lieutenant Maynard of HMS *Pearl* was sent to hunt Blackbeard down.

Maynard hid his men below deck and Blackbeard jumped aboard to kill him. That's when Maynard's force leapt out of their hiding places.

Maynard killed Blackbeard in a famous hand-to-hand fight. It's said that Blackbeard was shot five times and stabbed another 20 times before he finally fell. His head was cut off and stuck on the mast.

His body was thrown overboard and it was said that the headless corpse swam round the ship three times before it sank.

✖ DID YOU KNOW…? ✖

Blackbeard fell in love with 16-year-old Mary Ormond and made her his fourteenth wife. (He was a popular man.) He sailed off in 1618 and left her in Portsmouth. He never returned. (He couldn't. He was dead.) They say her ghost wanders the cliff tops looking for his ship.

Caesar

Nothing to do with Julius Caesar! This Caesar was an African slave who ran away and joined Blackbeard's crew in the Caribbean.

He was one of the few men Blackbeard really trusted and he was given an order...

When Blackbeard was shot and stabbed in 1718 Caesar hurried to blow up the ship as he promised. But two of his pirate shipmates stopped him.

Caesar was caught and hanged along with the others.

William Duell – who didn't die a pirate death:
Duell was hanged in 1740 at Newgate Prison in London. His body was cut down and taken to the doctors to be cut up. (They wanted to experiment to see how the human body worked.)

This was an extra punishment that pirates feared – they believed they couldn't go to heaven in bits.

The doctors washed Duell's body ready to start carving ... then noticed he was still breathing. Two hours later he was sitting in a chair. He was sent back to Newgate Prison, then transported to America.

💀💀 DID YOU KNOW...? 💀💀

A ghastly tale is told of a ghostly pirate ship. Late one night in October, 1864, a US ship was ready to set sail. Louis Billings, the master of the small ship, was getting ready to raise the anchor when he was frightened by a shriek from one of the crew. He reported...

A strange, old fashioned schooner with a big black flag was rushing down at us. She was on fire with a sort of weird, pale blue light that lighted up every nook and cranny of her. The crew was pulling at the ropes and doing other work, and they took no notice of us. They didn't even glance our way. They all had ghastly, bleeding wounds, but their faces and eyes were those of dead men.

The man who had screamed had fallen to his knees, his teeth chattering as he gasped out a prayer. I rushed forward, and told the crew to start saying any prayer they knew suddenly the schooner vanished before my eyes.

Some say that it was the ghost of Jean Lafitte's pirate ship, The Pride, that sank off Galveston Island in 1821 or 1822.

You may think it was a bad dream or a lie. But that same ship was seen again in 1892 in the same place with the same crew.

Interesting Index

Hang on! This isn't one of your boring old indexes. This is a horrible index. It's the only index in the world where you will find 'vomiting cows', 'mopping-up brains', 'pickled heads' and all the other things you really HAVE to know if you want to be a horrible historian. Read it and creep.

keel-hauling 50–1
marooning 8, 50, 55
mouth bolts 80
shooting 50
whipping 49–50

Quelch, John (pirate) 61

Rackham, Captain Jack (pirate) 31, 45, 70
ransom, holding to 31, 39
rats 5, 52, 66, 75
Read, Mary (pirate) 7, 44–5
Red Sea 83
Romans 23, 42–3, 49

Sadie the Goat (pirate) 43–4
St Patrick 23–4
scurvy 67
sea rovers 14
sharks 9, 80
Sharp, Captain 29
shellfish 50–1
Silver, Long John (character in *Treasure Island*) 69
skeletons 9, 70, 79
skulls 9, 16, 41, 44, 67, 69, 71
slaves 8, 13–14, 18, 23–5, 29–30, 63, 83
slops 65
snakes 16, 73
Snelgrave, Captain 67
South Seas 29
Spartacus (Roman rebel) 42
sugar 8, 25, 29
superstitions 75

swabbies 66

Teuta, Queen (pirate) 23, 43
Tew, Thomas (pirate) 71, 83
throat 13, 82
tongue 21, 66
torture 21, 44, 63, 74
treasure 5, 8, 14, 29, 31, 39–40, 52, 55, 58–9, 73–4, 76, 83, 89
'Treasure Island' 69

'USS Enterprise' 88

Venezuela 84
Vikings 11–12, 23, 42, 47
vomiting, cows 30

Wall, Rachel (pirate) 60
water-skiing 80
weapons 32–8
weevils 73
whip, lashes of 49-50
wine 28
Worley, Richard (pirate) 69
Wynne, Emanuel (pirate) 71